COVERED BRIDGES

RAPPS DAM BRIDGE ②

SHEEDER HALL BRIDGE ③

THE FOUR SEASONS
OF CHESTER COUNTY
VOL. II

THE FOUR SEASONS

Red Hamer, Author — Photographer

Rose-Marie Hamer Collins, Illustrator

*This Volume features
the complete all-color portfolio
of Chester County's storied covered bridges
and reflections of one of the world's
Greatest Horse Counties*

*Published by
Four Seasons Book Publishers
Red Hamer, Owner — President
P.O. Box 0222
West Chester, PA 19382*

OF CHESTER COUNTY II

BLESSING OF THE HOUNDS — Pickering Hunt, Thanksgiving Morning, in Chester Springs.

First Printing — 15,000 Copies — October, 1988

ISBN NUMBER 0-9605400-4-0
Printed By
Taylor Publishing Co.
Dallas, Texas

CAUGHT IN THE ACT — "Catch me if you can," says Mr. Reynard, who contemplates his next move at Seven Springs Farm in Chester Springs.

Foxes and Stuff

Throughout the development of this book my ongoing obsession was to capture a mature red fox on film.

Oh, the shooting of the pup (seen on this page) was fun. We just tossed raw hamburger down a fox hole and ten minutes later the kit ate his way to the top. The little critter was curious enough to be tamed.

But the mature red fox is something else. Fox hunters brought them over from England to Centreville, Md. in the 1700s to embellish the native gray fox. Predictably, they have made a habit of running from horses and humans in red coats. And humans with red hair.

I must confess that running through the fields with the Pickering Hunt was an exercise in futility; I *always* arrived five minutes after the fox.

Then along came Chris Murray, who appears on Page 62 and 63 as a decoy carver and hunter, with a solution. Chris transported a red fox to the Seven Springs Farm in Chester Springs for the devourment of my Canon AE-1.

But what you see on the facing page and page 65 is not what you think you see. What you see is a shelf fox. After it modelled for me, it went back onto Chris Murray's shelf.

That fox is stuffed.

And that will have to do until a real one slows down.

● ● ●

Ora Le Carr managed the Dilworthtown Country House gift store. The forecast was for snow, so I asked Ora to place her Santa Claus in the old sleigh across the parking lot when the flakes began to fly. Ora looked out her bedroom window at 4 the next morning and the snow had already covered the ground. With her robe flying in the sub-freezing breeze she hauled Santa onto the sleigh to set up the 10 A.M. shooting with my grand-children, Michael and Jessica Johnston, who fussed with Santa's beard on page 93.

Michael and Jessica agreed to a repeat performance in front of the Hayes Clark Bridge at King Ranch where they exchanged dandelions (pages 34-35). We then took a walk over to the nearby Mary Ann Pyle Bridge and came upon a piece of luck. Frolic Weymouth and friends were having a

AUTHOR, AUTHOR . . . Focus on an inert animal.

carriage picnic on the hillside (page 30-31). The four white horses made a striking picture as they turned for the covered bridge.

● ● ●

Frolic's Chadds Ford estate The Big Bend, and Ronde-lay, owned by the Ambassador William Hewitts, served as additional backdrops for carriage activities (pages 6-13). The actual Battle of the Brandywine was fought at both sites.

Pat Theurkauf, secretary of the Pickering Hunt, introduced us to all of this horsey activity. "Chester County has more horses than any county in the world," she professed.

Don and Judy Rosato, of Chester Springs, are winners of the prestigious coach and four competition at the Devon Horse Show (p.17) and authorities, it seems, on every carriage and sleigh known to mankind. The old world charm of their sport as reflected in their impeccably appointed St. Matthews Place (circa 1715) on pages 66 and 96 and their contagious enthusiasm accounts for so many carriage and sleigh photographs, the spillover to be displayed in a Volume III, I am sure.

— Red Hamer

SPRING

HERALDING IN SPRING — Alexander Hewitt drives his family's coach and four to the entrance of their Chadds Ford home, Rondelay, for a gala spring carriage party.

RONDELAY — they came in all kinds of carriages from sulkies to elegant coaches dating to the turn of the century to this very unusual 1984 spring party at the home of William Hewitt, U.S. Ambassador to Jamaica, and Mrs. Hewitt, of the Deere tractor family. Foundation of the former Brinton homestead dates to sometime between 1680 and 1720.

ANDREW WYETH (dark gray cape at left) America's best known artist, lives across Rt. 100 from Rondelay, which was built in its present form about 1820. The former Quaker residence was a haven for runaway slaves.

FROLIC'S BASH — George (Frolic) Weymouth, at the reins of red carriage (above) built in 1894, kicks off his annual carriage party the weekend of the Winterthur Races. The 250-acre Chadds Ford estate takes its name, The Big Bend, from the Lenni-Lenape Indians' description of the Brandywine River which makes a big hook there. "William Penn was granted the land in 1683," noted Frolic, "but he deeded it back to the Indians. They used it as a trading post."

Upwards of 60 carriages and more than 200 driving enthusiasts annually display their carriages over the artistic trails of The Big Bend, pictured over the next four pages. Exhibitions are also held at Winterthur, Delaware that first weekend in May, and the Cheshire Point to Point, Unionville, in the fall.

MAIN SECTION of The Big Bend (above) was built in 1750. Weymouth, who purchased the estate in 1960, is a former seven-goal polo player. He has owned more than 100 carriages but gave most of them away.

SCENES ALONG THE BRANDYWINE from fishing, to canoeing to rafting into the rapids are taken in by the footmen aboard a carriage (center). Nearby the terrain climbs dramatically to provide a hilly meadow (right) for a grazing horse.

JOURNEY CONTINUES through The Big Bend country . . .

. . . AND WINDS UP back at the barn for a horsey smooch, a washdown, a cocktail and some idle chatter.

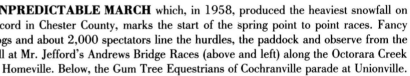

UNPREDICTABLE MARCH which, in 1958, produced the heaviest snowfall on record in Chester County, marks the start of the spring point to point races. Fancy dogs and about 2,000 spectators line the hurdles, the paddock and observe from the hill at Mr. Jefford's Andrews Bridge Races (above and left) along the Octorara Creek in Homeville. Below, the Gum Tree Equestrians of Cochranville parade at Unionville.

... TO POINTS

DEBORAH ROCK FARM (above and at left), owned by the late State Sen. Thomas P. Harney, was the backdrop for the Brandywine Point to Point near Marshalton before that race was moved. At left, below Jock Hannum watches son Jeb win Junior Race at his grandmother's Cheshire Point to Point, Unionville. Buzz Hannum, below, brother of Jock, weighs in after winning Winterthur Bowl in 1984. Jeb, checking scale, was Delaware Valley Rider of the Year in 1988, the same year his uncle Buzz broke five ribs in the Maryland Hunt Cup.

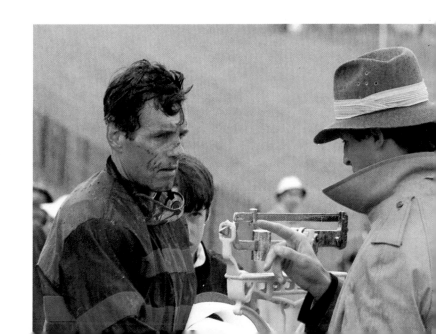

WINTERTHUR POINT TO POINT is featured on pages 18-19.

EASTER SUNRISE SER-
VICE at Brandywine Battlefield State Park, Chadds Ford.

Devon Horse Show

THE DEVON HORSE SHOW has evolved over its 90 years into a great equestrian, social and shopping event. Olympic and world equestrians compete for the Devon blue in 34 divisions every spring, but some of the more popular and successful competitors come right out of Chester County.

WHAT MORE GLORIOUS SIGHT than raw equine muscle, with gay colors aboard, surging over hurdle after hurdle on a beautiful early May afternoon at Winterthur, Delaware. Thus, the 1987 edition of the meeting which annually concludes the Chester County Point to Point spring season. 8,500 tail-gaters attended.

THIS TIME WARP SETTING out of the 19th century is Green Valley Farm on very rural Apple Grove Road, halfway between Coatesville and Unionville. Home was built in 1827, the barn in 1820. The Jenny family, current owners, found it to be perfect for their veterinary business. Most of horse and cattle grazing is on pitched hills (page 21).

AMISH COUNTRY is quite visible on the perimeters of Chester County. Just drive west of Coatesville on Rt. 30 and turn right on Rt. 10 and you will observe scenes like the children (above) waiting for their parents at the country market, or the young men scrubbing down their buggies the day before Easter, or plowing a field the old fashioned way.

EMBREEVILLE ROAD HOUSE (page 24) on Route 162 along the Brandywine. Too hidden for the Revolutionary War to find it, this 1760 structure with a walk-in fireplace makes a pretty picture in spring. The Wilson Reynolds, the owners, run the Embreeville feed mill next door.

VILLAGE OF MARSHALLTON was named after botanist Humphrey Marshall (1722-1801) whose National Historic Landmark home (at right) he built in 1773. It lies next to Marshallton Nursery (above). The 19th century sled was built for the heavy snows of Falmouth, Maine from which it was exported. Marshall authored two important books on botany. One or two trees in the front yard may have been planted by him. Chester County Historical Society was bequeathed the 50 acres of his estate, which once numbered 350 acres.

THE KISS OF THE SUN
FOR PARDON
THE SONG OF THE BIRDS
FOR MIRTH
ONE IS NEARER GOD'S HEART
IN A GARDEN
THAN ANYWHERE ELSE
ON EARTH

SPRINGTIME-IN-WEST CHES-TER garden tour blends the color, fragrance and fresh paint of April at 9 W. Lafayette St. former carriage house (circa 1830) above and the 11 W. Biddle St. townhouse (c. 1803) at right. The sign at 127 Elbow Lane tells it all.

SERENITY AND OPEN BEAUTY of <u>SOUTHDOWN</u> catches the motorists' eyes along Rt. 162 between West Chester and Marshallton. Gilbert Cope (1840-1928), who helped to found the Chester County Historical Society and wrote a monumental history of the county with J. Smith Futhey, was born here. His father brought over Southdown sheep from England from which estate got its name.

SCHOOL'S OUT at Amish farm house near Parkesburg.

29

PENULTIMATE PICNIC at Mary Ann Pyle Covered Bridge (originally built in 1881). With John M. Seabrook, of Woodstock, N.J. at the reins and Frolic Weymouth, of Chadds Ford (turned down hat) as his guide, antique carriage heads home after an unusual country picnic at Kings Ranch, April of 1985.

THE 15 COVERED BRIDGES
of Chester County

GIBSON-HARMONY HILL Covered Bridge (c.1872) is a beauty from any angle. Located on busy Rt. 322 between Downingtown and West Chester, it is seen by more travellers than the 14 other county covered bridges. The East Brandywine Creek span was named for a local farmer, George Gibson.

MICHAEL JOHNSTON, of West Chester, presents dandelions to his sister, Jessica, on a lovely April, 1985 day at the *Hayes Clark Covered Bridge* on the King Ranch. Floods from Buck Run destroyed earlier editions of this bridge as with its twin, Mary Ann Pyle, one-quarter mile away. Fire consumed the bridge again in 1963, but it was rebuilt in 1971. The privately owned twin bridges are admired for, among other things, their beautiful stonework.

AUTUMN BECOMES BARTRAM'S covered bridge, which spans Crum Creek and enjoins Chester and Delaware counties. It was built in 1860, closed to traffic in 1941 and restored in 1970.

Below, silo and barn along nearby Crum Creek Road, and another view of creek which empties into Springton Reservoir.

LARKIN'S COVERED BRIDGE has literally been put to pasture. Former site of the span is under 60 feet of water of Marsh Creek Lake.

Bridge was built in 1854, rebuilt in 1881 and moved in 1972 to this northern and remote part of recreation area.

DOUBLE DIP . . . These two nags are of one mind on a warm autumn day downstream from Sheeder-Hall Covered Bridge, the **38** oldest (1850) and northernmost of the county's 15 covered bridges. Spanning the French Creek, it enjoins East and West Vincent Townships.

CHESTER SPRINGS is where the sleighing action is and the Sheeder-Hall Bridge is right in the middle of it. Steel runners skim through the 116 feet of wooden planks hardened by cold.

BELIEVE IT OR NOT the fisherman hooked a fish while the young tubers were sailing down Valley Creek toward the KNOX COVERED BRIDGE this summer day in 1985. The Valley Forge span, first constructed in 1851 and again in 1865 after a flood destroyed it, is the most photographed and painted covered bridge in Chester County.

RAPP'S DAM BRIDGE (above) and KENNEDY BRIDGE (below) are only a mile apart as the crow flies and located just north of Kimberton. They also span French Creek. Rapp's Dam has its original 1866 marker and survived heavy damage by Hurricane Agnes in 1972. Kennedy (c.1856) is a meeting place for students at Kimberton Farms School. It was torched in 1987, rebuilt by the county in 1988 at cost of $400,000.

TO THE EAST of Oxford and Nottingham and clustered near the Maryland border are three covered bridges: Glen Hope (left), Rudolph and Arthur (center) and Linton Stevens (below).

GLEN HOPE (c.1889) was torched in 1987 but rebuilt in 1988 for $250,000. Original cost: $1767. It spans Little Elk Creek while Rudolph and Arthur (c.1880) and Linton Stevens (c.1886) cross Big Elk Creek, both of which empty into the Chesapeake Bay.

THE LONG ONE ... Pine Grove Bridge's two spans extend 204 feet across the Octorara Creek between Chester and Lancaster counties. Both photos were taken from the Lancaster County side. Stage coaches regularly crossed on what was an early national road between Philadelphia and Baltimore. Level of dam was raised in 1950 to pump water 40 miles to city of Chester.

WHY DO ROOSTERS CROSS THE ROAD? . . . To get a better view of Mercer's Ford Bridge (above and left). Span (c.1880) crosses Octorara Creek between Lancaster and Chester counties about a mile south of Atglen.

SPEAKMAN'S BRIDGE (c. 1881), located to the north of two other covered bridges on the King Ranch but open to the public. Beside bridge are ruins of a mill first built in 1844 by Jonathan Speakman. Bridge lies nestled between steep hills of the area.

SWEET STRUMMIN' at Old Fiddlers Picnic, Hibernia Park.

SUMMER

FIDDLIN' AROUND . . . Fiddlers are everywhere, and in all heights, widths, ages and sexes from the band stand to the woods at the 56th annual Old Fiddlers Picnic, at Hibernia Park, August of 1984.

A FAMILY AFFAIR . . . While fiddlers from as far away as Florida and as near as Chester County were doing their thing, the square dancers and their young 'uns were doing theirs at the West Caln Township grounds. Cecil Miller's Oxford Rythmn Boys (above) had the 10,200 sun bathers dancing and clapping. Hibernia is part of the 2,223 acre park system in Chester County.

ILLUMINATED EVENING fountain displays have become an annual summer-time treat at Longwood Gardens since 1931, witnessed yearly by 200,000. This Festival of Fountains display in 1984 was preceded by an Al Raymond big band concert indoors. The water — sometimes accompanied by fireworks and always by music — is jetted 130 feet in the air while over 700 lamps tint the water in various hues of color. And it's all done by computer.

LONGWOOD GARDENS, near Kennett Square, was the summer home of Pierre S. duPont (1870-1954). The industrialist personally designed the 1,000 acre estate and filled it with horticultural and hydraulic wonders that have made the gardens and fountains the most lavish in the United States.

The Lights
of Longwood

HOT PINK coordinates Festival of Fountains display (left page) with carousel and botanical gardens flower arrangement — and Lynne Hamer's sweater — at Longwood Gardens.

SHIMMERING WATERS . . West End Swim and Tennis Club on Rt. 842, West Chester, makes a lovely summer retreat.

CHADDS FORD DAYS — Quilts and wooden bowls are among the wares for sale during the early September celebration that raises funds to preserve and hold activities at such historical buildings as the John Chad House (c. 1725) and Barns-Brinton House (1714). Chris Sanderson kicked off the first festival in 1958 with his famous fiddling depicted by internationally renown Chadds Ford painter Andrew Wyeth. 15,000 attend the two-day craft, art and entertainment show.

OFFICERS' QUARTERS (c. 1777)

BATTLE OF THE

OPEN-AIR CLASSROOM — Re-enactment of the Battle of the Brandywine draws kids and grown-ups to state park along Rt. 1 during Chadds Ford Days weekend.

SERENE VIEW of Brandywine Battlefield Park from a high perch.

BRANDYWINE

CHESTER SPRINGS GRIST MILL — Almost 200 years ago, not just the water of Pickering Creek sparkled. Mill was center of activity along Yellow Springs Road. It is part of Millbridge Farm, owned by Mrs. Sandy Heilman.

'WELCOME TO AUTUMN, I THINK' — says *Spot*, the welcoming committee at Dr. Edward and Pat Theurkauf's 100- acre Lone Pine Farm, Elbow Lane, Chester Springs.

LONE PINE FARM — is the handsome backdrop of a mother and daughter Saturday morning ride (Mrs. Pat Theurkauf on right with daughter Ann). Part of the Elbow Lane, Chester Springs house pre-dates 1740.

RIDE THROUGH HISTORY — Dr. Don Rosato and wife Judy pass Yellow Springs Inn while riding with the Pickering Hunt. On September 17, 1777, soon after the Battle of the Clouds in Chester County, Gen. George Washington slept at the inn.

SETTING FOR AN ARTIST . . . Chris Murray, 1984 Chester County Decoy Carver of the Year, could not have selected a more artistic place than Seven Springs Farm on Lower Pine Creek Road, Chester Springs, to display his work. The West Pikeland Township showplace has an original 1779 core, seven levels, a friendly ghost, 18-inch walls and 15 owners prior to Bob and June Holman.

OVER THE HILL — a man and his best friend, on the hunt.

BEAVER FARM — located 4 miles west of Phoenixville on Seven Stars Road; first settled in 1712 by Jonathan Rogers who lived in cave and wrestled the Lenape Indians in pasture above, according to farm's 60-year tenant Clyde Scheib, on tractor (right), who led fight to restore nearby Kennedy Covered Bridge in 1988. Main stone house started out as log cabin in 1793. Gen. Washington's entrenchments to prevent British from seizing his iron furnace at Hopewell are discernible here. Red maple (page 65) was planted in 1928, when Scheibs first leased 110-acre crop and dairy farm from the Beavers.

VIEWS AT THE TOP — Chester Springs and St. Matthews roads (page 66) is one of the highest elevations at about 800 feet in Chester County. The bikes are along a fence at Larking Hill Farm and that's Melanie McCardle riding her Clarabelle.

ON A DIFFERENT level of St. Matthews Road is St. Matthews Place (c. 1715 says the sign), home of Dr. Donald and Judy Rosato, and assorted felines. Long porch leads to barn full of horses and antique sleighs and carriages.

NOT ALL OF THE BEAUTY is inside the botanical gardens at Longwood Gardens. This red maple directs you down the road to the front door.

GLENN COOPER fires off 'Brown Bess', a British musket, to start a heat of the autumnal tradition Marshalton Inn Triathlon, 1985 edition. Meanwhile, Northbrook bridge spectators and pooch are silhouetted while watching canoe portion of peddle, paddle and pace competition.

CHURCH FARM SCHOOL never looked lovelier than framed by an autumn-blazed old tree in early November. 1988 plans called for school to remain, but over 1,000 of its acres to be commercially developed by Rouse and Associates along Rt. 30 corridor in West Whiteland Township. ONE-ROOM SCHOOLHOUSE turned residence (left) on Pine Creek Road, Chester Springs.

VINCENT BAPTIST MEETING HOUSE (above), Art School Road, Chester Springs, erected in 1812, enlarged 1852; **WEST VINCENT TOWNSHIP BUILDING** (right) is the former Birch Run Schoolhouse built in 1863. Pitch of the hills in this area creates scene not uncommon to Vermont.

JOURNEY'S END FARM is a showplace in wide-open East Nantmeal Township along Templin and Hollow Roads. The horse farm was adding to its 40 stalls in 1988. It offers training in dressage, show-jumping and cross-country jumping. Field stone house in background (top photo) was built in 1769, owned by Richard A. Moore, farm's original owner.

STUFFED SHIRT WELCOMING COMMITTEE along Rt. 113 as one enters Chester Springs from the south.

AMISH HARVEST along Barnsley Chrome Road between Oxford and Chrome in southwestern Chester County, leads right to the barn across the street. Pockets of Amish line the Octorara Creek on the county's western boundary right up through Honeybrook where 90% of the farm land is owned by this very special culture.

GEESE ALONG MARSH CREEK LAKE flying into winter

THE HUNTSMAN — Wesley R. Bennett (top), professional huntsman for the Pickering Hunt, gathers the hounds before the morning charge through the woods. Pickering was chartered in 1910 and for 40 years William J. Clothier, Jr. a former national tennis champion, was its master of the hounds.

THE RED FOX was brought over from England to Centreville, Md. in the 1770s because the local gray fox did not provide enough sport for the hunters.

"The gray fox will only run in a small circle. The red fox will strike out and run for miles in a straight line," explained Mrs. Pat Theurkauf, secretary of the Pickering Hunt. But the goal of the hunt is not to kill the fox, but to observe it.

A SERENE BRANDYWINE bordering artist Andrew Wyeth's estate along winding Rt. 100, Chadds Ford.

FROZEN MARSH CREEK LAKE near Eagle silhouettes cross country skiers at sundown.

WINTER

APRIL SNOWSTORM in 1982 turned this Hickory Hill barn on Rt. 472 four miles southeast of Oxford into an art study.

CHRISTMAS at Dilworthtown Country House is a fantasy land for Jessica and Michael Johnston, of West Chester, who examine Santa's beard outside and marvel at the toys inside. Michael also makes a wish at the window.

WEST CHESTER PUBLIC LIBRARY (above and at right) at N. Church and Lafayette Sts., West Chester, looks more like a castle as it turned 100 years old in 1988. THE ZOOK HOUSE (below), circa 1734, adjacent to the Exton Square Mall.

CLAUDE RAINS HOUSE — late actor's home at 400 S. Church St. (above) and neighbor's 103 Dean St. Victorian house (left).

CHESTER COUNTY HISTORICAL SOCIETY building (above) designed as horticultural hall in 1848 by Thomas U. Walter; left, Mrs. John D. Flagg's c. 1807 spring house at 1021 Fern Hill Road, West Goshen.

FAIRVILLE INN c. 1826, attractive in daylight, takes on a magical hue in early evening before a light carpet of December snow. FAIRVILLE VILLAGE (below) has antique shops to attract the Rt. 52 customers, and a snow laden barn across the street.

WAYNEBROOK INN (below) is the cornerstone of Honeybrook. Original structure was built in 1738. Former Bull's Head Tavern was drawn on the British War map because prominent Honeybrook residents actively opposed the crown.

DULING-KURTZ HOUSE AND COUNTRY INN (above) dates to 1830 as the main house of a grist and saw mill business in Exton. It was named for the mothers of Raymond Carr and David Knauer, the inn founders. PEDDLER INN, c. 1870, is located in Honeybrook; STOTTSVILLE INN (below), including bar, c. 1858, Parkesburg. Presidents Grover Cleveland and Benjamin Harrison slept there.

PINE CREEK MILLS and its seven dwellings on Lower Pine Creek Road, Chester Springs, is always as pretty as a picture, no matter what season. Two buildings were saw and grist mills c. 1750. Stone house on right dates to 1801 where Joseph M. Clement, noted illustrator for the Saturday Evening Post, once lived. Pine Creek becomes Pickering Creek one mile downstream, eventually flows into Schuylkill River.

COUNTY SEAT all dressed up for Christmas: West Chester Friends Meeting c. 1868 (left); geometric S. Church St. home fronts (below).

LINCOLN BUILDING (above) and Lorgus Flower Shop (right), Market St., West Chester.

JINGLE OF THE BELLS is almost audible in this
breath-taking sleigh ride through new-fallen snow in

BIRCHRUNVILLE STORE, built in 1898, in the heart of Chester Springs' sleighing country. Roads are snow covered until 10 A.M. when the salt and cinder trucks arrive, although sleigh enthusiasts have been known to attempt to dissuade the trucks from their appointed rounds.

DASHING over the fields with Dr. Donald J. and Mrs. Judy Rosato. The Owen J. Roberts mansion, home of the late Supreme Court justice, is in the background. Inset: hand and rein action as sleigh heads toward mansion.

93

CRISP JANUARY TEMPERATURES and a half foot of new snow make for perfect sleighing, tubing and tobogganing along School House Lane at West Vincent Township building (this page) and through entire Birchrunville (right page) where a picnic atop mountainous hill tops off the day. Antique sleigh dates to 1890.

HOME IS WHERE THE BARN IS, in this case at the Rosatos' St. Matthews Place in Birchrunville. After the tack is put away and the horses led to their stalls, the winter fun retreats to a fireplace where refreshments and perhaps a video of the day's events are served up.

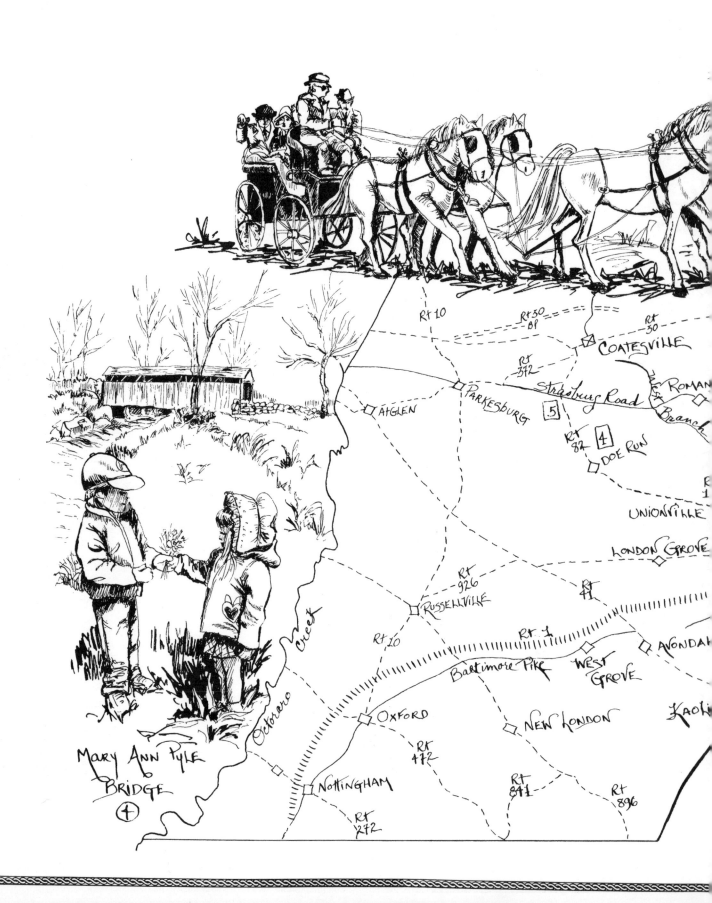

Rt 10
Rt 30
BP
Rt 30
COATESVILLE
Rt 372
Strasburg Road ROMAN
PARKESBURG 5 Branch
ATGLEN Rt 82 4 DOE RUN
UNIONVILLE
LONDON GROVE
Rt 926
Rt 41
RUSSELLVILLE
Rt 10 Rt 1 AVONDALE
Baltimore Pike WEST GROVE
Octorero Creek OXFORD NEW LONDON Kaoli
Rt 472
MARY ANN PYLE
BRIDGE NOTTINGHAM Rt 841 Rt 896
4 Rt 272